ELON Under the Oaks

Photography by Will & Deni McIntyre with a foreword by President Leo M. Lambert

ISBN 978-0-9679506-3-1

ISBN 0-9679506-3-5

Photographs © 2005 by Will & Deni McIntyre

All rights reserved. No part of this book may be reproduced or transmitted in any form or by any means, electronic or mechanical, including photocopying, recording, or by any information storage or retrieval system, without the written permission of the Publisher.

Published by Loose Ends Press™

3746 Yadkinville Road

Winston-Salem, North Carolina 27106

www.macfoto.com

Printed by Harperprints

Design by Anna Dancy

ELON
Under the Oaks

by Will & Deni McIntyre

Foreword by President Leo M. Lambert

Dear Karen,

Thank you for your service to the Elon community. I send very best wishes on your birthday!

Leo Lambert

October 2, 2007

The Oak

Live thy Life,
    Young and old,
Like yon oak,
    Bright in spring,
        Living gold;

Summer-rich
    Then; and then
Autumn-changed,
Soberer-hued
    Gold again.

All his leaves
    Fallen at length,
Look, he stands,
Trunk and bough,
    Naked strength.

- Alfred, Lord Tennyson

Brushstrokes in Maroon and Gold

All of us who love Elon, at whatever age in life, share common sensory experiences about this special place: familiar brick walls and archways…the brilliance of a warm, mid-April day…oak trees in new leaf and dogwood and azalea exploding in color…the quiet of prayer during chapel in Whitley Auditorium…the warm sunshine of commencement mornings…light and shadow on the Alamance cupola…an office window – maybe your favorite professor's – lighted late into the evening…the sounds of Alumni Gym packed with noisy fans…the strains of the Fight Song on a football Saturday…the particular scent of library books.

Older members of the Elon community remember lovingly places that exist now only in memory and history: the Senior Oak…basketball in old North Gym with the balcony sometimes blocking your shot…men living in the Publishing House and women residing in Ladies Hall…driveways at both entrances to Alamance, with parking for day students… newlywed life in Vets Court…times enjoyed between classes in the fraternity and sorority rooms in Mooney Building.

Recent years have added new delights to the campus landscape: Fonville Fountain's dancing water…Tuesday College Coffee on Scott Plaza…classmates strolling through graceful colonnades bordering Young Commons…Belk Library, lighted in the late evening, filled with students…all of us on campus, finally, for fall football games in Rhodes Stadium…almost always a crane or a construction fence somewhere…air-conditioned residence halls wired with 21st century conveniences (a far cry from the days of the Publishing House!)…modern, up-to-date science facilities in McMichael. Everywhere, on a campus more than a century old, there is a sense of newness: scores of committed new faculty and staff joining experienced colleagues…new buildings blending well with older ones given new leases on life…new dreams built upon proud accomplishments… excellence in the air.

Remembrances of the sights and sounds and even scents of places stir us deeply. This book captures images of a place we love, but I hope it will spur even more important remembrances of the people who were important to you during your time at Elon: a professor whose expectations challenged you to reach higher than you ever dared…a turning point in your life when someone at Elon tapped you on the shoulder and pointed you in an exciting new direction…a mentor who is still one of the most influential people in your life today. You will undoubtedly remember friendships that to this day bring warmth to your heart. Maybe you were even so fortunate as to fall in love at Elon.

It is the nature of looking back to mark what has changed. What is more important, however, is to mark what has endured at Elon: an unwavering commitment to engaging students and connecting their learning to the world around them…a commitment to an education that transforms mind, body, and spirit…a commitment to maintaining a sense of community that is palpable even to first-time visitors…a commitment to the finest liberal arts tradition…a commitment to preparing leaders who will work toward the common good on this earth. This is our mission, and we will forever be devoted to carrying it forth.

Graduates of Elon College, graduates of Elon University, Fightin' Christians and Phoenix, faculty, staff, students, parents, and friends, join me in the great chorus that proclaims "Long live Elon!"

Leo M. Lambert
President

10   New Student Convocation

An acorn for each new student

President Emeritus Dr. J. Earl Danieley

Overleaf: Isabella Cannon International Studies Pavilion and Ella Darden and Elmon Lee Gray Pavilion

Alumni brick on Young Commons

Center for the Arts at twilight

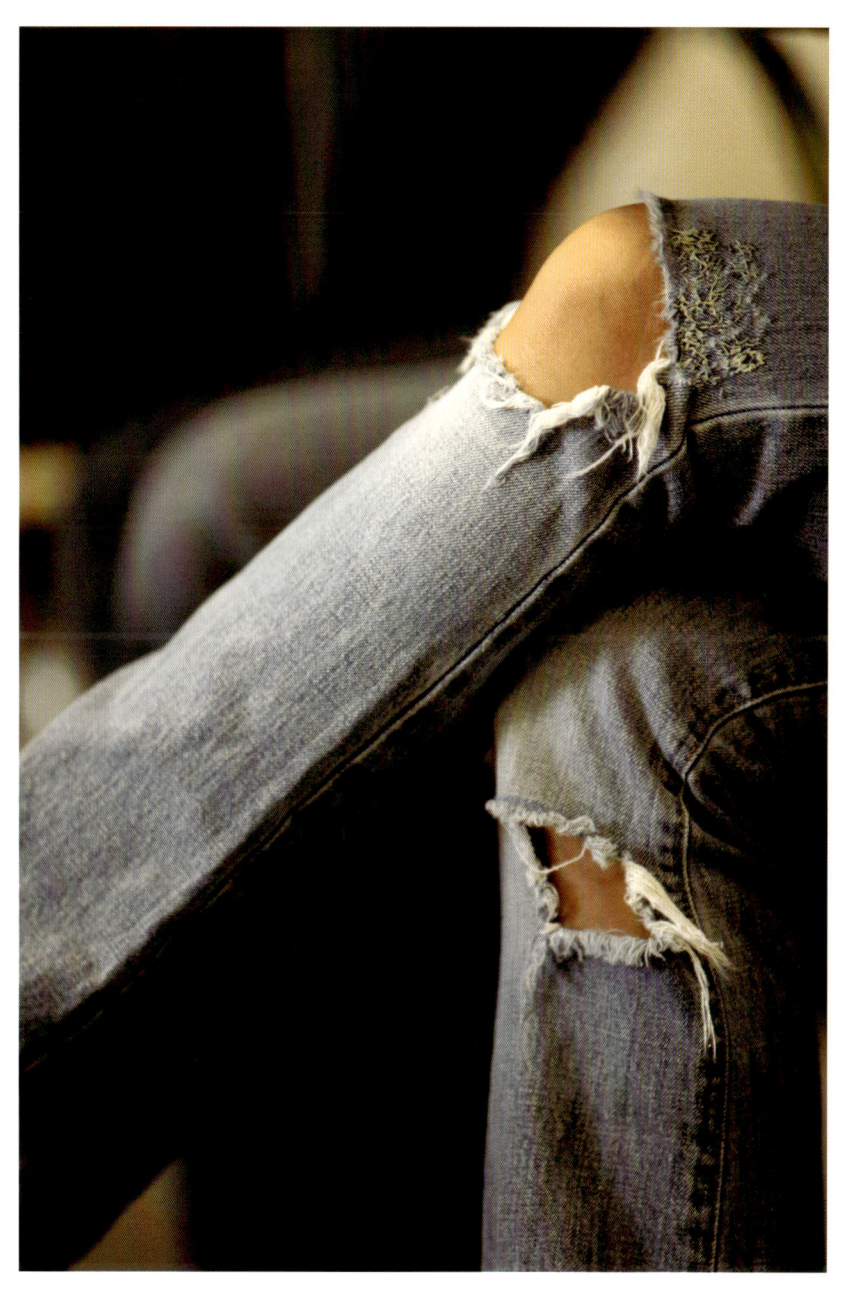

School of Communications television studio

McEwen Dining Hall at night

Other Elon residents

44   In the library

Life in Sloan Hall

Preceding page: Homecoming fireworks over Moseley Center

50

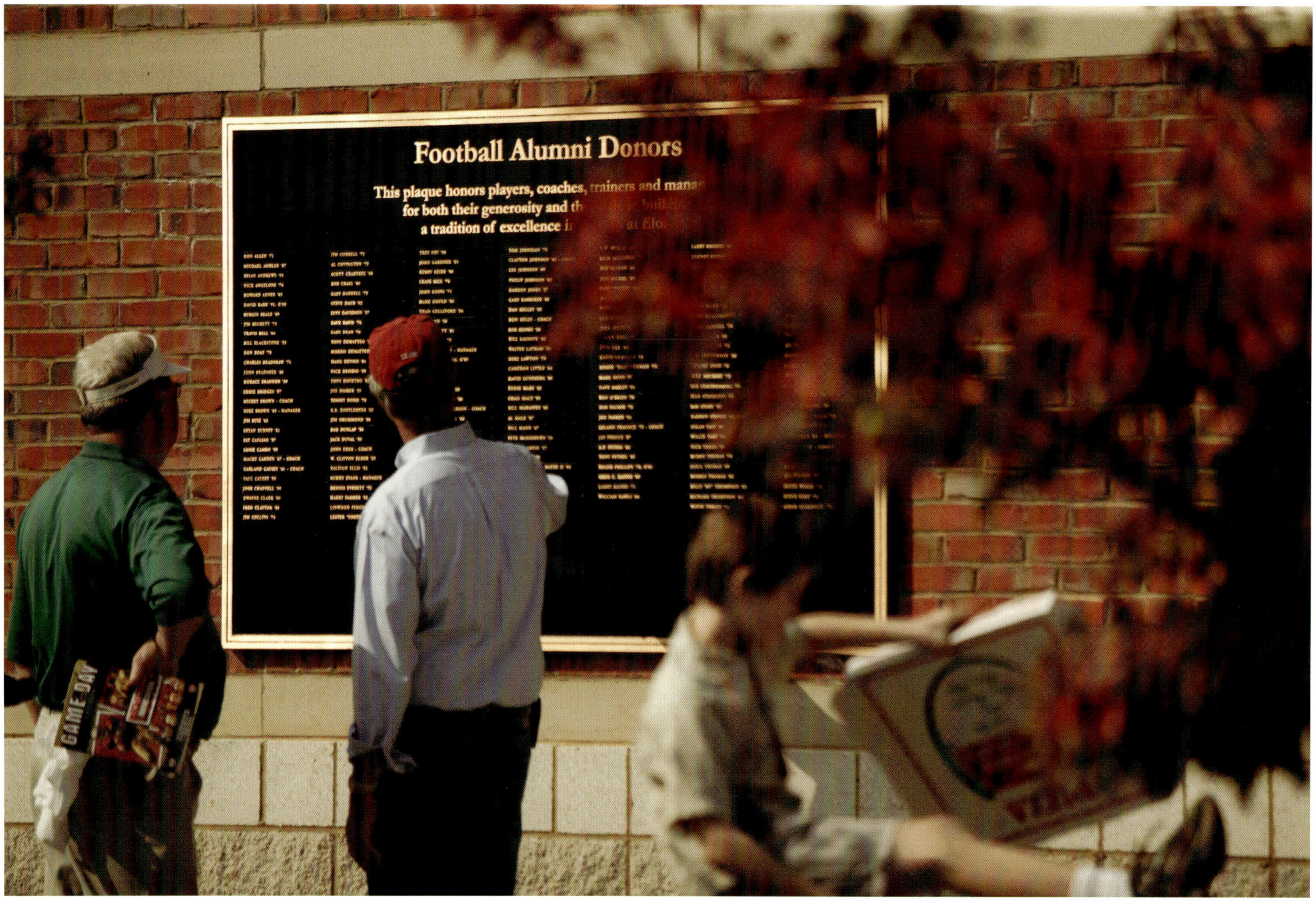
Football Alumni Donors
GAME DAY

GO ELON!

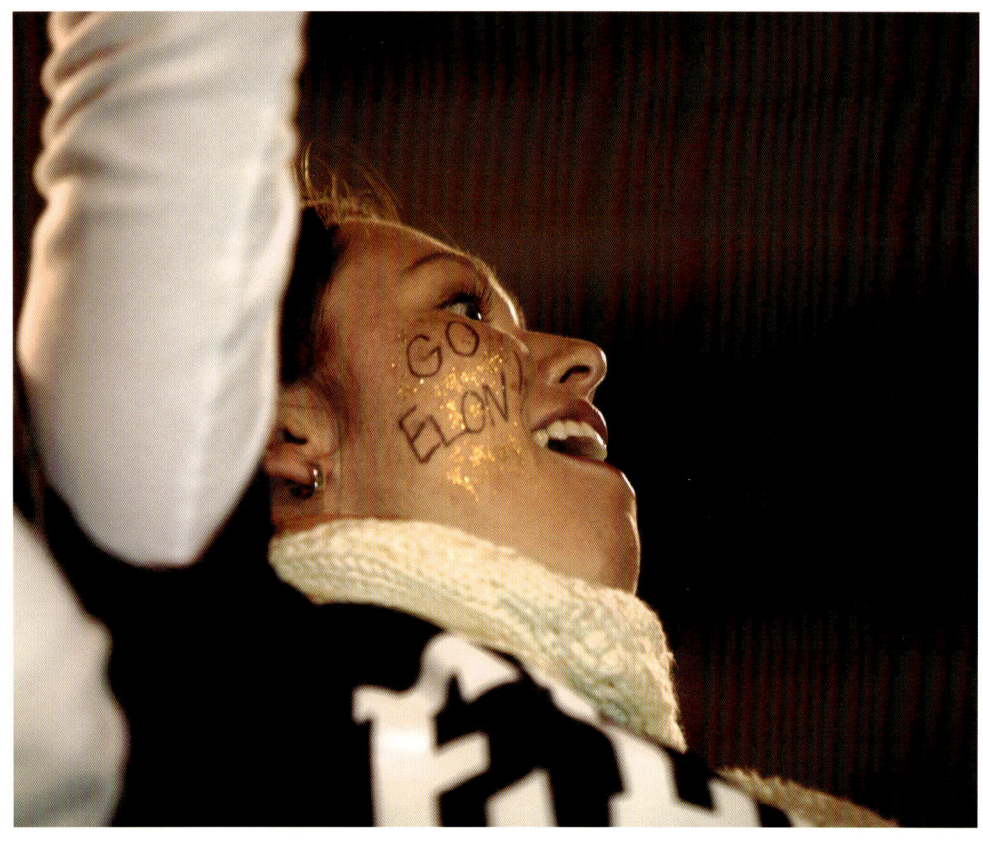

Colonnade between Whitley Auditorium and Carlton

In the rare book collection

Casavant organ in Whitley Auditorium

Evening concert

Whitley Auditorium

Overleaf: Carol Grotnes Belk Library in winter

Christmas decorations at Jordan Center

Rotunda in Alamance

Going home for the holidays

Bell Tower   Top: Phoenix Rising sculpture, detail

View from Alamance balcony

Dalton L. McMichael Sr. Science Center

Carol Grotnes Belk Library

Fonville Fountain, Alamance and Long

Sidewalk outside Koury Center

A Convocation for Honors 103

Jimmy Powell Tennis Center

Whitley Auditorium balcony

Belk Library skylight

Previous page: Walter C. Latham Park

Loy Center

118 College Coffee at Fonville Fountain

119

122   Finals Week

The Acorn Coffee Shop on Williamson Avenue

128   Commencement

Long Live Elon!

134 Reflection of Alamance in a punch bowl

An oak sapling for each graduate

Acknowledgments

Thanks from Will and Deni McIntyre
to the following friends and acquaintances whose
enthusiasm and expertise helped shape this book:

Daniel Anderson
Denise Briles
Matt Eviston
Gerald Francis
Chelsea Johnson
Sarah Johnson
Leo M. Lambert
Candace Midgett
Leigh Miller
Carolyn Nelson
Nan Perkins
Kathy Scarborough
Jerome Sturm
George Troxler

Also, thanks to everyone who appears in these pages.
Your generous cooperation and encouragement gave us
a new appreciation of the community that is Elon.

"Remembrances of the sights and sounds and even scents of places stir us deeply. This book captures images of a place we love, but I hope it will spur even more important remembrances of the people who were important to you during your time at Elon …"

— From the foreword,
"Brushstrokes in Maroon and Gold,"
by President Leo M. Lambert

ELON
Under the Oaks

The Elon community and the timeless beauty of the campus are celebrated in an exquisite new book titled *ELON Under the Oaks*. This limited edition hardcover book includes 137 color photographs that chronicle life on the Elon campus, from move-in day and fall colors through the beauty of spring and Commencement.